TRACELESS

Exploring the spirit of fell running

little peak press

Traceless – Geoff Cox & Heather Dawe

First published in 2020 by Little Peak Press

www.littlepeak.co.uk

This book is a work of fiction and non-fiction. The non-fiction sections are based on the life, experiences and recollections of Geoff Cox and Heather Dawe. In some limited cases the names of people, place, dates and sequences or the detail of events have been changed solely to protect the privacy of others. The authors have stated to the publishers that, except in such minor respects not affecting the substantial accuracy of the work, the contents of the book are true.

Edited by Jo Allen

All illustrations by Heather Dawe

Background cover photograph by Andy Jackson, inset cover photograph by Geoff Cox

Design and Production by Rhiannon Hughes, www.theyorkshirewordwright.co.uk

A CIP catalogue record for this book is available from the British Library.

ISBN: 978-1-9160812-3-9

FSC
www.fsc.org
MIX
Paper from
responsible sources
FSC® C005094

Printed and bound in the UK

TRACELESS

Exploring the spirit of fell running

Geoff Cox & Heather Dawe

little peak press

Gerry Charnley is little remembered, but was a prolific fell runner, orienteer and climber who founded the Karrimor International Mountain Marathon (KIMM), now the OMM. He died tragically on Helvellyn in his early 50s. To commemorate his memory, his friends established his namesake Round.

Light on the Crinkles

The Charnley Round is a 38-mile clover-leaf route that consists of 26 checkpoints centred on the Charnley Cairn close to Esk Hause in the central Lakeland fells. The checkpoints are not peaks, but map features and places of interest, and three are youth hostels – Eskdale, Borrowdale and Langdale. The Round can begin anywhere, but is normally started from one of the hostels. It was designed to be run or walked in one long day, and for loops and linear routes to be completed as the runner chooses. The ethos of the Round is self-sufficiency and leaving no trace – the runner is encouraged to plan their own route to visit all the checkpoints, then to navigate that route, creating their own line from multiple route choices.

Contents

1 : TRACELESS --- 11

2 : INTRODUCTION -- 12

3 : BORROWDALE -- 19

4 : AS WATER FLOWS – Part 1 ----------------------------------- 28

5 : GERRY CHARNLEY ROUND – Attempt 1 -------------------------- 32

6 : NIGHTFALL AT CHARNLEY CAIRN – A Story --------------------- 38

7 : AS WATER FLOWS – Part 2 ----------------------------------- 48

8 : MAP READING --- 50

8 : GERRY CHARNLEY ROUND – Attempt 2 -------------------------- 53

10 : AS WATER FLOWS – Part 3 ---------------------------------- 58

11 : WHY TRACELESS? --- 62

12 : TRACELESS DAYS --- 68

ACKNOWLEDGEMENTS --- 73

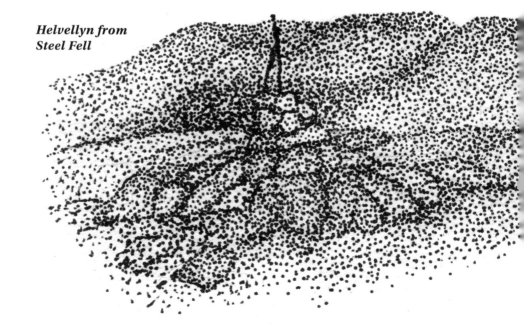

Helvellyn from Steel Fell

Traceless

Heather

Your mind is at one
with your body and the land around you
Map in hand, brain translating the contour's swirls and circles
into shape, solidity, three-dimensional reality

The studs on your shoes leave marks
that will quickly fade back into the land
Nothing else will show you
Nothing else can see you

A run that will soon be a memory
Nowhere else
Traceless

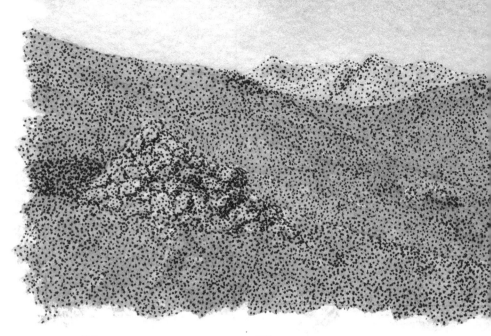

Looking to the Langdales from Silver How

Introduction

I was in Canada when Geoff first mentioned the Gerry Charnley Round. I'd heard of it before – thought it was something I would like to do some time, but never got around to finding out much more about it.

The conversation with Geoff took place on Twitter in autumn 2019, when with a few others we were discussing the merits of guidebooks for challenges like the Bob Graham, Paddy Buckley and Ramsay Rounds. I'd suggested, only partly tongue in cheek, that maybe we should each go for a long run, not tell each other where we'd been and argue in the pub afterwards whose run had been tougher. 'That sounds like the Gerry Charnley Round,' responded Geoff. A seed was sown.

Two weeks later, back in the UK and staying at Borrowdale Youth Hostel for the night with my mum and my two daughters, there was a coincidence that helped the seed to grow. In a corner of the dining room, neatly folded in a clear Perspex box, were a number of maps entitled 'The Charnley Way'. I had stumbled upon the first printing by Harveys of their Gerry Charnley Round (GCR) map. I picked up a copy and unfolded it. There before me was not only a map of the Round, but also a biography of Gerry Charnley – about the man and what led his fell running and orienteering friends to create the Round in his memory. Truly a piece of history. Along with these main details were adverts for the Karrimor International Mountain Marathon, Tanky's Trog, and the Capricorn and Saunders tents. Fell runners of a certain age (I just about get over the line here these days), will fondly remember these events, and that kit, as absolute classics.

Geoff certainly gets over the line. I sent him a photo of the map (the YHA staff kindly let me take away a copy), and within a day he got back to me with the idea for this book.

Here we are a year later. Plans for long runs around the Charnley Round decimated by a pandemic that grounded us all, so instead Geoff and I delved into our memories. No matter, memories can be sustaining things and I even turned my hand to writing fiction.

Heather, September 2020

I first heard of Gerry Charnley in 1981, while I was working as Warden of Bell Cottage, high in the Greenside Valley above Glenridding in the Eastern Lakes. Every week I'd host a couple of police officers from Greater Manchester, and around a dozen young people who were deemed to be 'at risk', for a full-on programme of outdoor activities. The young people usually coped well with the pace; the police officers often less so, and I heard myself being compared to Gerry on a number of occasions: "You're like that Sarge Charnley, he's not got a bloody off-button either!" I never met Gerry, but find it poignant that those conversations were happening just a short distance from where he fell to his death the following year. He was working as a police instructor, sharing his skills and experience with a group of cadets on a snow-swept Helvellyn edge.

Despite being a regular competitor in events like the KIMM and Lowe Alpine Mountain Marathon (LAMM), I don't recall hearing Gerry's name until I read an article about running the Gerry Charnley Round by top Lakeland fell runner Ben Abdelnoor in the autumn 2007 issue of *Fellrunner* magazine. Ben described it as "a grand day out" so I logged it as 'one to do' (to be taken at a more leisurely pace than Ben had adopted).

On the shortest day in January 2015 I unexpectedly ran into Ben. We were both working on the Marmot Dark Mountains, an overnight mountain marathon which was that year being held in the Howgills. Between sending competitors on their way out into the cold hostility of a winter night, I chatted to him about the GCR and picked up on his enthusiasm for something that was "a bit different". It moved status to 'one to do soon'.

At that time I was putting together a plan for my 60th birthday celebrations and the conversation with Ben helped crystallise what that would be. I decided that I would run the 'three named Lakeland Rounds' (the Joss Naylor Lakeland Challenge, The Bob Graham Round, and the Gerry Charnley Round) in my 60th birthday year.

And what a year that was! An obsessive and emotional roller-coaster filled with friends, fatigue and so many wonderful days running the hills I love. When it all came to a close the 'year of highs' was replaced by a massive burden of anticlimax, which I found very hard to deal with. The mental hangover induced by the emotional effort of completing these rounds sat in my head. A stifling layer of concrete that I knew I had to crack. I decided what I needed to do to deal with the aftermath was to write an account of the three runs. After several false starts I realised that expressing my thoughts and feelings in prose wasn't working. To my surprise and embarrassment I found myself writing poetry!

The three poems I wrote, one about each of my three long runs, formed the narrative of the film *Trailpike* that my great friend Rich Berry and I launched into the world in 2017. Or rather, two of the poems did. 'A Shepherd's Hand' and 'Twenty-Three and a Quarter, Clockwise' formed the basis for the film. In truth we ran out of money before we could do justice to the inclusion of 'As Water Flows'. The poem languished in my computer until I found myself drawn into a Twitter conversation that, among others, included Heather.

During that conversation I recognised in Heather somebody who wasn't scared of expressing an opinion, and many of those opinions were closely aligned to my own. The Gerry Charnley Round is something rather special in the context of fell running – it isn't a line on the map that must be followed

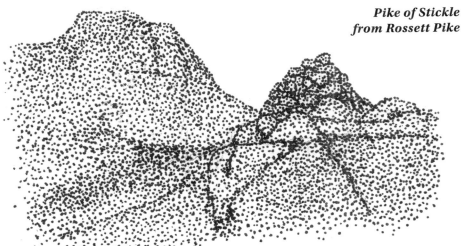

*Pike of Stickle
from Rossett Pike*

to register a success, it isn't a sequence of fell-tops that must be gained within a set time, it isn't an expression of strength and dominance – it's simply a collection of places that, accurately navigated between, provide the basis for a wonderful day (or days) in breathtaking scenery. I knew that those shared views might be a place where Heather's talents and my poem might meet, so I hit the 'send' key and hoped she might feel the same enthusiasm for a joint project.

That project is this book. 'As Water Flows' has found a home at last, adorned with Heather's beautiful and evocative artwork, and a collection of our other writings and images that we've loosely gathered around our passion for the hills, and thoughts about hill-going. The run conceived in Gerry Charnley's memory connects them all. We hope that you enjoy our explorations of what it is to be 'Traceless'.

Geoff, September 2020

Borrowdale 3

It was drizzling at the bus stop outside Booths in Keswick. A grey day, but although you couldn't see the summit of Skiddaw from the centre of town, wrapped in cloud as it was, the lower tops were clear to see. The north-western fells were silhouetted in progressively lighter shades of grey. Barrow, Oughterside, Grizedale Pike, Causey Pike – all just about free of clag. Over the past few days I'd been staying in Braithwaite, the village nestled at the bottom of Coledale, with my family for a week just after Christmas and into New Year. While there I'd taken every opportunity to run over and among these local fells.

That morning, instead of running on these fells, I wanted to run the Borrowdale Loop of the Gerry Charnley. Twelve miles or so, starting from the youth hostel at Longthwaite, initially climbing Glaramara, to Allen Crags, the Charnley Cairn, Angle Tarn, Stake Pass, and then returning to the youth hostel down the great valley of Langstrath.

While I'd been hoping for a clear day, it was not to be. Standing at the bus stop, I wondered what the day was going to bring. It was the kind of weather where the grey could easily be blown away, replaced by sunshine and showers. Equally, the way the cloud felt sunken, maybe I would rise above it as I climbed into the central fells, break clear of it into the perfect blue sky and bright sunshine of a temperature inversion. I was hoping for the latter.

The bus stop was busy with walkers. As we left Keswick and made our way up the valley, the bus became progressively emptier as we each reached the beginning of our various trips out into the fells and along the valleys of Borrowdale.

Combe Gill

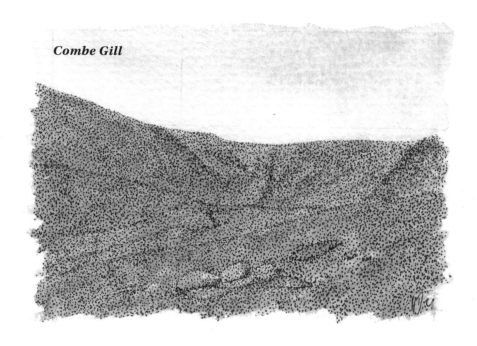

I got off the bus near Stonethwaite, at the stop closest to the youth hostel. I ran towards it along the little road that leads to Thorneythwaite Bridge and then past the hostel, along a footpath following the young river Derwent. After a mile or so I crossed the river and the road up Borrowdale to another footpath to begin the climb up Glaramara.

This path winds its way through and up some fields before joining a big new track up into Combe Gill. There was a significant amount of work going on in this little valley, I assumed to mitigate flooding. Borrowdale has the dubious honour of being the wettest place in England. During the Christmas floods of 2015 there had been lots of damage, both in the valley and down river in Keswick and Carlisle.

The little valley I was running up is Thorneythwaite, in which a subsidiary beck to the Derwent forms high in the fells and then flows down to join the larger river. When I just passed the sheepfold on the other side of the gill, about halfway up the valley, I knew it was time to climb, to leave the path along the gill and head up towards Glaramara taking a direct line.

It had been a year of no racing for me, the first in over 20 years. Not only was I not race fit, I'd not navigated in the mountains much that year and not at all at a racing speed. Although I was not racing, I was running and remembering to pay heed to the map was something I needed to tell myself to do. Navigating at any kind of speed in the hills requires you to keep in touch with the map. By this I mean always knowing where you are on the map, something particularly important in low visibility as this can make it extremely tricky to stop and relocate if you lose it. This kind of running in the hills requires concentration. Along with holding my location and line, I also find that translating the map to the shape of the terrain from the map to the ground and attempting to 'feel' it around you can really help. I had missed this kind of running and thinking; it was good to be doing it again.

The clag sat tight on the upper tier of Combe Gill. The whole time I was climbing, I had been secretly hoping for an inversion, when you leave the clouds below you, layered like the sea, the hills above forming islands basking in sunlight. The last time I'd experienced such an inversion was on the eastern edge of the Cairngorm Plateau the previous January, climbing a few of the Ben Avon summits with my partner Aidan. Back then we left the mist about 300 metres below the summits – emerging to see the whole of the plateau in an ethereal kind of light. The cloud did become a little less dense as I approached the summit of Glaramara but the inversion was not to be. I resolved to enjoy the mist and the challenges it brought.

Before Glaramara I needed to find Clatter Crag, a small hilltop with a cairn a few hundred metres east of the path. I delighted myself by taking a compass bearing and heading straight to it, even in that clag – despite such little practice that year I could still do it. At that point I told myself not to get too smug – next time I could easily make a mistake unthinkingly, especially if I started to believe I was some navigation ace.

Two days before this, I'd run up Grizedale Pike in the north-western fells. It had been very windy at the summit – as I descended that mountain towards Coledale Hause I was cushioned by the wind, leaning into it I could feel my face becoming misshapen by its force. It was windy on Glaramara – not that windy, although I did nearly get blown over at the summit. I saw the cairn and shelter next to it and ducked in to get out of the wind enough so I could check my line off the top.

Taking a bearing using my thumb compass, I held the map folded small in my right hand, pressing the compass to it, looped as it was over my right thumb with its elastic band. Most orienteers use thumb compasses, certainly those who race, something I had picked up from them. Different to the traditional compass with its plate and bezel, a thumb compass enables you to more closely keep the map and compass connected, and to quickly orientate yourself to a change in direction by simply turning the map in your hand.

I lost the path among the crags and rock-strewn summit of Glaramara. I had taken a bearing to the next checkpoint, High House Tarn, and just ran on this, over tussocks, rocks, occasionally weaving between crags.

The clag was now dense; it was windy and raining. Increasingly the doubt began to set in as I ran. What if I'm going completely in the wrong direction? What if I overshoot or just totally miss High House Tarn? What's my back-up decision? At this point I was entirely reliant on the map in my hand and the compass; the only other things with me were my hand-wound watch and my phone, but the battery had just died (I had brought it along to take photos). The wind was flapping at the map gripped tightly in my hand – *if I lose it now I'm stuffed; I should have put a spare in my bag...* I did think at this point that an altimeter would have been useful. I rarely use one, but they really show their value in conditions like these I was running in. Stubborn to the last, I wanted to do this run in the way I interpret to be 'properly', a map, compass and no other gadgets.

It felt lonely, running through that cloud. While close to the path, I wasn't on it. I could have tried to find it, but that felt like a waste of time, particularly as on the boggy ground I was crossing it might just be more of a faint broken trod than something distinct and reassuring. I felt like I was passing across the fellside completely alone (and I was), but there must be a few others nearby in the Central Fells of the Lake District, despite the weather. At that point I didn't really want to see anyone to speak to, just to be reassured by the presence of someone other than myself on the fellside. I asked myself what I would do if I came to the conclusion I had completely lost my way. The response? *Find a safe line north-eastwards off the fell into Seathwaite.*

However, despite my self-doubt and feelings of loneliness, the thing about following the compass on a bearing as governed by the map is that it is an entirely rational, objective thing. I knew where I was when I had taken the bearing – the summit of Glaramara. Hold true to the bearing and it will take me to High House Tarn, give or take 20 metres or so. Furthermore, even if I overshot everything, I would hit a big track on the perpendicular, on the other side of Allen Crags in around three kilometres. At that point I would be on one of the main highways of the Central Fells and if I wanted to, I would not have to leave it until I was back in the valley at Stonethwaite, half a mile from the youth hostel. Once there, I could work out exactly where I was, find myself the security of an established way, and keep to it for the rest of my time out on the fell. This is what I told myself anyway. Even so, I still felt lonely and full of self-doubt.

Unnamed Tarn

I knew I was running on a ridge from both reading the map and having run the line before – quite broad, but a ridge nonetheless. I wanted to get to a position where I could feel the land dropping away to my right more steeply than the relative flatness of the ridgeline to my left, to feel the shape of the land around me. This was my line – where the objectivity of map reading and the subjectivity of mountain going come together. That feeling is a state of flow, *the* state of flow I have come to love when running in the mountains with a map in my hand. If I can shake the feelings of loneliness and self-doubt, what actually shines through when I am doing this is one of joy, exhilaration, sometimes maybe even euphoria. At one with my body, mind, the map in my hand and the fellside, I am running free through the mountains, my most loved places where I get closest to truly being myself.

Just as I was beginning to believe I'd missed the tarn it appeared from out of the gloom, the large flat greyness of its water contrasting with the darker land surrounding it. The tarn was exactly where it should have been according to my bearing, which miraculously I had held as I moved this way and that between the crags and boulders in my way as I ran off Glaramara. I shouted with glee to myself and the hillside – not only had I managed to navigate to the tarn, this meant I now knew exactly where I was, which was a relief. I hadn't dwelled on it, but in the back of my mind I had begun to wonder how I would find myself if I didn't hit the tarn or the track a kilometre or so beyond it. That is the nature of mountain navigation in weather like this – such faith has to be placed on the bearing; I always have to remind myself to keep to it when my head begins to pull me in slightly other directions.

Again I told myself not to be smug – all too often I have made mistakes soon after navigational successes such as this, arrogance subsequently getting the better of care and attention. I kept to the same bearing I had taken off Glaramara, which should take me directly over the summit of Allen Crags and then down to the large path junction at Esk Hause. From the tarn the ground started to gently rise, just as it should do according to the map. I followed the line. Eventually the ground began to descend, which confused me as I'd not seen the summit of Allen Crags. However, I soon found a large path more or less on my bearing and followed it to the col. So I had missed the summit, but found the path that leaves it – *that'll do*. Someone was sitting in the shelter just below Esk Hause, at the top of the path to Angle Tarn. I didn't stop to speak to them, but kind of appreciated their presence.

The next checkpoint was at Esk Hause, after which I would climb for a little while towards Esk Pike before contouring westwards towards the Charnley Cairn. I thought of Gerry as I ran – I was eight when he died and never got the chance to meet him, but I bet he relished the challenge of orienteering in conditions such as those I was running in.

It was a slow, rocky traverse. I was due to meet Aidan and our daughters back at the youth hostel in just over an hour and a half and so I was pushed for time to do the full loop I'd planned. While I came close to the Charnley Cairn (I'd been there before in similar conditions), I didn't stop to try to find the plaque; I planned to be back there soon, hopefully in better conditions when I would look to properly find it. From close to the cairn I traversed in descent towards Ore Gap, the small col between Esk Pike and Bowfell. I was heading towards Angle Tarn, backtracking along a line I had taken just over two years earlier, with my friend and running partner Andrea Priestley during the Original Mountain Marathon (OMM). The 50th anniversary event. I think the planner Joe Faulkner ensured that every competitor would visit the Charnley Cairn, celebrating one of the people who established the event back when it used to be the Karrimor. In clear weather the views from the cairn are expansive – the Sca Fells, Upper Eskdale, the Duddon – so many of the Lakeland's finest fells and such a grand location for a memorial.

At Ore Gap I again backtracked the route we had taken on the OMM, first traversing downhill towards the path that climbs to Esk Hause from Angle Tarn, then descending this large stepped track to stepping stones at the mouth of the tarn. From there I reversed a line I had taken so many times during fell races and my own runs in the hills. I recalled memories of both the Langdale Horseshoe and Old County Tops races as I followed the path that would take me all the way to Stake Pass, the col that separates the two mighty Lakeland valleys of Langdale and Borrowdale.

Visibility steadily improved as I lost height. After a couple of kilometres I had dropped out of the clag and could see around me and where I was heading. After the stepping stones at Angle Tarn, Stake Pass was the next checkpoint. The path I was on followed the wide ridgeline to the col, curling eastwards and coming steadily closer as I made my way along, passing a few walkers going in the opposite direction.

As I ran, I remembered the second time I did the Old County Tops fell race in 2013. Of all the Lakeland fell races I think this shines through as my favourite. A classic test of fell racing and endurance, it is also an aesthetically beautiful route that visits the three highest points of the historic counties of Westmorland, Cumberland and Lancashire – Helvellyn, Scafell Pike and the Old Man of Coniston respectively. Seeking to regain my previous levels of fitness and endurance after having my first baby, I had found the race tough, breaking a bit after Cockley Beck on the long, rough, steep haul up towards the Old Man. The race is for teams of two and I was again running with Andrea Priestley. On the long section linking Helvellyn and Scafell Pike we'd made the race harder for ourselves by losing the line to Stake Pass during a traverse along the western side of High Raise, overshooting it, ending up down in Langdale Combe and having to climb back out. I remember seeing runners trotting along the good path that crosses Stake Pass on the skyline as we climbed back out of the Combe, swearing at my nav error, frustrated with having to climb more than we should have in order to regain the route.

This time by myself I reached Stake Pass, marked as it is by a small unnamed tarn, a little cairn and a crossing of paths, without error. I didn't stop for the view but kept running hard, at pretty much race pace to get down off the fell quickly and not be late for Aidan and the girls. What constitutes race pace for me these days is somewhat slower than it used to be. As I ran along I smiled to myself – this was the closest I had come to racing for quite some time. Instead of testing myself against other runners I was racing the clock, for reasons other than trying to beat something or someone. While Aidan would not be angry if I was late (maybe fairly cross if I was especially late), I appreciated the time he had given me to run on the fell and did not want it to seem otherwise.

In all my 20 years of running in the central Lake District I have rarely travelled down its large valleys, instead sticking to the ridgelines and summit approaches above. From Stake Pass the path zigzagged down into upper Langstrath, a series of tight hairpins like some mini Alpe d'Huez. I did the traditional fell running thing of cutting out these turns by running steeply down the side. I know that defeats their purpose, but old habits die hard.

As I descended into the valley I could hear the dull roar of fast-moving water – all the rain of the last 24 hours quickly leaving the fellside, heading down to form the Derwent and eventually travel out to sea. It was raining harder now. Despite it getting warmer as I got lower and into the valley out of the wind, I kept all of my waterproof gear on, quickly becoming very warm even though soaked through.

The path on the eastern side of the beck where I was running looked rockier and less defined than the one on the western side. As I ran along it I debated crossing the water to what looked like faster ground. Is it always the case that the other path looks better, the grass seems greener? I was trying to work out whether the time and faff it would take me to cross the beck and onto the other path (which could be just as rough going) would be less than the time I saved by a potentially faster path or whether I should just stay put and keep going.

I kept going, eventually crossing the beck close to Black Moss Pot. I was then on flat, faster ground, running hard to where Langstrath Beck meets Greenup Gill. I then had less than two miles to go, following the path to where it becomes a road at the village of Stonethwaite and along it some more back to the hostel. I was not particularly late after all.

I shouldn't have worried about Aidan and the girls being bored while they waited for me. They had tea, pop and cakes from the bar in the hostel and were ensconced in the games room playing table tennis, having spent their morning exploring the beach and coastline at the seaside of St Bees. After changing into some dry clothes, I got my own tea and cake and joined in the fun.

As Water Flows – Part 1

Geoff

A silent village, a morning bridge, and swallows,
new born from night-cooled roosts,
glean flies above the wakening stream.
To hills where slate and blasting charge
have shaped the land and scored broad ramps
by handrail walls through heathered tops
the first delights of the day ahead.

And on I flow,
as water flows,
unchanneled.

Blea Water, still. A foliate frame around
an old glass mirror, polished with use.
Sunrise hills, inverted wedges
driven deep into liquid blue.
The molten gold of fellside bracken
spills through wall gaps in green intakes
where sheep cast wool and indifferent stares.

And on I flow,
as water flows,
warmed by the morning.

Sweat beads, salt to tongue and eyes.
Vague trods braided into rocky crag and combe.
Height gained slowly, won against
the downward ooze of Blisco bog.
A spring flower opens, Red Tarn, a bowl of blue.
Reed-fringed pool furnished with grass couches,
a place to linger, to feed the body and relax.

But I must flow,
as water flows,
shoulders to the sky.

Crinkle Crags, deep shadowed door and tenuous
step, then pillared halls of columned stone
from Long Top to Three Tarns,
where two valleys merge and coalesce
and route decisions must be embraced.
My way's for the Esk, and the river emerges,
shining and scaled like an adder's back.

And on I flow,
as water flows,
drawn to lowlands.

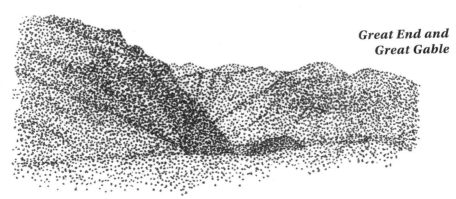

*Great End and
Great Gable*

Langdale

5

Gerry Charnley Round, 2015, Early May Bank Holiday, Attempt 1

Geoff

It was light early, although it felt more like autumn than early May. There was a sparkle of ice on grass and leaves; the river had that brittle sound that comes with frost and cold conditions.

I didn't know how many to expect – clubmates had said that they'd turn out, but from experience their enthusiasm rarely survived the reality of an early start. I thought I could count on the stalwarts – Martyn and Helen, Tom and Penny, Andy Jackson – but beyond that...?

Ten minutes before we're due to start and it's looking more like bank holiday Blackpool than Elterwater. Twelve have turned up – everyone I'd expected and a whole bunch of others. I groan silently at the thought of holding this together and say something to them that I hoped would be both motivational and a warning to the weak – this had the makings of a long day in so many different ways.

The customary countdown and we're off, down the leaf-hung lane out of the village. Within 200 metres we're off-route, but everybody is relying on somebody else to navigate, so nobody notices. It's only when the trail turns downward and clearly this isn't the summit of Lingmoor that the rush stops and we look at each other with sheepish grins. Backtracking would be sensible, but the idea of forcing a route up through boulder field and forest is mooted and, with silence being taken for consent, we're off up into terrain that is distinctly runner-unfriendly. At one stage the whole party teeters along the top of a huge and moss-draped wall looking for any trace of a

Eskdale

likely uphill path. Eventually we spill out of the woods, scraped, sweaty and well down on schedule. Inwardly I give myself a good talking to; it's good to be out with such a high-spirited team of friends, but mistakes like this are both embarrassing and potentially dangerous.

Lingmoor checked. Down the badly eroded path to Blea Tarn, which offers gorgeous reflections in the stillness of morning. Blisco, Red Tarn and then the heart-in-mouth sight of 12 runners demonstrating a wide range of confidence and competence in ascending the Bad Step up onto the Crinkles. After a lifetime of outdoor instructing I can't help but count them when we get onto the ridge. Still 12 and all accounted for.

The view from the top is breathtaking, but to the west we see the first signs of changing weather. The forecast was a change for the worse, but had been ambiguous about where and when the change would be felt. From up here, there doesn't seem to be any doubt about it – we're in for some bad weather, and soon. I think of the route ahead and start my pace and time calculations, thinking what's to come.

Any worries are set aside for the laughing charge down the Upper Esk on paths that were made for fast running. We collect the two valley checkpoints, ascend some steep and precipitous stiles, and drop onto Eskdale tarmac under increasing cloud. I'd spoken to the youth hostel team to arrange tea and cakes, so we're met with a smiling welcome (admittedly under a raised eyebrow as the size of our party is significantly more than I'd suggested on the phone). Refreshed, with good luck wishes ringing in our ears, we spill out into what feels like a different season. It's cold; skies threaten rain or worse, and everybody goes through a mental checklist of the weight compromises they made when packing for the day.

A short spell on tarmac then it's up the long Terrace Route drag towards the improbably large boulder on the shoulder of Slight Side. We don't make it before the weather front hits us hard; heavy sleet on a keening wind sends everybody diving for waterproofs and extra layers, but it's an exercise in awkward, one-legged hopping and soon it's clear that we need to work together, forming a ring to shelter those in the middle
still struggling to dress. Emperor penguins
in head-to-toe Gore-Tex.

On past the giant boulder, a scramble onto the summit crag of Slight Side then noses down for Scafell. By now it's full winter conditions, a blizzard that sees runners leaning at crazy angles into the wind while holding hoods close to frozen faces. I run through a list of who we've got here, who I know will handle these conditions, who are the unknown factors, an appraising look at the size of packs and the way people are moving. But we're pretty much staying together and easily regather at the summit cairn to check the bearing for the entrance to the gully down to Foxes Tarn. I know it's important that we get this right as there are three different people with compasses in their hands; this is no place for poor navigation.

Dropping into the gully is like closing a door on the weather. It's suddenly calm and quiet, significantly warmer than the summit. Plastered snow slides off packs and jackets and there's a marked relaxing of shoulders and faces. Thinking ahead I know that escape routes need to be considered; we're moving well now, but these conditions make for slow going. It's the Bob Graham route in reverse as far as Esk Hause, known ground, no need to tag every summit, but these are anything but BG conditions. Let's take stock at the Hause shelter and make some decisions there. If anything, the weather seems to have improved for this section so

Scafell Pike and Bowfell

I've recced this leg; I know the altitude reading for where we leave the path to traverse towards the Charnley Cairn and the number is written on my map. But in the lee of Esk Pike the snow has accumulated and now lies deep on the ankle-threatening boulder field that my line was supposed to avoid. I wipe the melting snow off my map with my thumb and realise that I've misread the elevation – we are way too low and potentially in a lot of trouble. It's painfully slow going and the slower pace means we chill fast; it's less than a kilometre, but it's a nightmare of slipping, sliding, sinking progress. Any chance of success disappears in that few hundred metres. Eventually the boulders thin out and we can feel grass under snow – there's a temptation to speed up, but not until after a consultation that ensures we hit the cairn first time.

This is no time for sentiment: Ore Gap, Angle Tarn, and down into Langdale on the Rossett Gill path is the prescription. It's time to take what the hills have given us and retreat to fight another day.

Nightfall at Charnley Cairn
A Story

Heather

She leaves the road to join the path at the foot of Hardknott, close to the point where the tarmac steepens to form one of the hardest climbs in the country to cycle. Memories of riding up it flooded through her – grinding away at the steepest points, trying desperately to stay on the bike, not to have to relent, to get off and push.

A warm evening; this time she is running not riding. 'Fast-packing' – that's what they call it these days. Whatever. She is heading into the mountains, a rucksack on her back packed with things for a night high among the fells. Sleeping like this, alone, is something she often dreams about, yearns for, particularly when she has not travelled into and across the fells for a while. The last time she ran in the mountains felt a lifetime ago (in reality it is only few months). The light and warmth of the evening is already making up for time away from them. It's not that her life away from the fells is bad, just busy. The occasional time spent in the mountains brings a sense of scale, reality, eventually tranquillity. As much therapy as it is exercise.

An old phone box, contrasting bright red against the greens, greys, browns and yellows of the fells, marks the beginning of the off-road. From there she will follow the Esk to its source, over Lingcove Bridge, under and up the side of the crags of Throstle Garth, past Sampson's Stones, along the great hanging valley of Upper Eskdale, under the high crag of Scafell Pike to the dale-head at Esk Hause.

It is early May and still smells like spring – while the day is hot, the evening will become colder. Along with her sleeping bag, she'd packed thermals and a down jacket to sleep in, a little stove for a hot drink before she falls asleep, and to brew coffee for a morning fix at daybreak. The excitement she'd felt when bringing together and packing her kit had been palpable – she was heading back to the high fells to spend a night up amongst them.

The path starts climbing very gently up the valley, river still wide even though she's close to its source. The fields full of lambs a couple of months or so old. They'd lost that skippiness and amusing inquisitiveness and were on their way to turning into mature Herdwicks. Turning the continuous wheel of growing and ageing, soon to learn the ways of the fells from the older sheep of their flock.

After a mile or so, once through the fell-gate, the ground around the path is rougher. She runs on, looking up the valley. Wide to begin with, it narrows just upstream of Yew Crag. With the narrowing the river flows faster, the waterfalls and deep pools the valley is renowned for moving white and fast. She'd jumped in a few of them some years before on a baking hot July day, when plunging into cold mountain water seemed the only sensible thing to do.

The path she follows past the pools leads to a fork in the river. Here the Esk meets Lingcove Beck, a tributary that rises under Crinkle Crags and Bowfell. Astride it sits Lingcove Bridge, the classic Lakeland crossing, stone set in place, an old packhorse way. Pausing a while to take a photo of the bridge, she then crosses over, imagining those who used it in times past, appreciating its craft and longevity.

Soon at Esk Falls the ground steepens and narrows, the path continues up the eastern side of the now fast-flowing river, forced into a tighter space by topography. She has always thought of the rocky buttress of Scar Lathing that sits at the head of these narrows as a fortress guarding a secret world. The great hanging valley of Upper Eskdale lies beyond, there to share its beauty and peace with those who venture up into it.

Hanging valleys are some of her favourite places, and Upper Eskdale the one she loves the most. Isolated and peaceful, the dark crags looming over its north-western side rising up from the yellow-green flat wetlands surrounding the young Esk.

Climbing the steeper ground, she slows to a walk. Fast-paced though, pushing down with her hands on her legs just above the knee. She wonders why she's trying so hard when no one else cares how fast or slow she goes.

No-one's racing today; there is no one here but me.

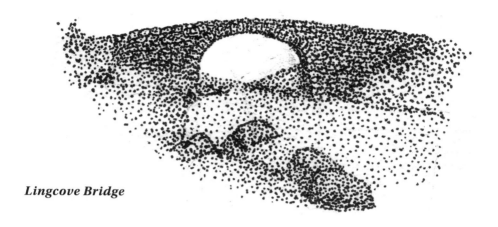

Lingcove Bridge

Beneath Scar Lathing the river turns sharply ninety degrees. The ground begins to flatten – she's close to Great Moss, the expanse of boggy ground that surrounds the river, forming the floor of Upper Eskdale. After a little more running, the river turns again and there she is, back in the place that had so absorbed her mind when she had painted the scene now opening up before her. Painting a landscape leads you to look so much. When you return it feels like an old friend.

The wonderful Sampson's Stones. Those cluster of boulders that form a perfect contrast to the rock cliffs beyond: little and large. She passes them by, remembering previous bivvies. Summer nights sleeping in their shelter, waking the next morning to climb rock routes on Esk Buttress.

Running on upriver the ground is flatter still. There is a peace about Upper Eskdale she only feels when here alone. This is why she yearned to come here, to get away to this different place whose age and remoteness brings a sense of perspective to the rest of her life. It's hard to explain the need she has to come here to those who have never felt this pull. Some of them think it's selfishness, others escapism. It's probably both of these, along with a hint of self-indulgence, but also something that helps her stay sane in a world that seems to be getting crazier.

She runs through the shadow cast by Esk Buttress. The day is beginning to end. Pressing on now to get up to at least the Hause by sunset, ideally to the summit of Esk Pike. At an easy spot to reach into a fast-flowing stream she fills up both of her water bottles. Hot chocolate when she is snug in her bivvy bag will be a luxury as she lies waiting for darkness.

The ground steepens as she approaches the Hause. She fast-walks again, pressing on to keep ahead of the closing light. Now the low sun is casting ever-longer shadows, marking out the folds, re-entrants and streams of the fellsides around her, just as she had hoped. Smiling, she feels like she has entered her daydreams. Just how she'd wished this evening would be.

At Esk Hause she pauses, admiring the stone walls of the four-pronged shelter, looking over to the Langdales, north to Glaramara, west to the great rocky outcrops of Broad Crag, Scafell Pike and Scafell. Further in the distance to the north-east, the outline of Saddleback sits on the horizon, dark mountain against pinky-red sky.

The climb to Esk Pike is gentle – the path winds through rocks and boulders. Summit reached, she again pauses to take in the view, and then heads off due south, not far until her resting place for the night, the Charnley Cairn. She runs faster, trying to get to the cairn before the sun finally leaves for the night.

Half a mile or so from the summit the ground becomes less rocky and the ridgeline she is running down begins to level out. As the trod becomes grassy, she knows she's approaching the cairn, slightly off to her right, upon a rocky ledge. Such a fine position, with expansive views west as the fells drop to the sea, north to the Scafells, south to the Langdales and the Coniston fells beyond.

Finding a perfectly shaped patch of soft grass with no rocks, she unrolls her sleeping mat and sleeping bag, laying them both flat within her bivvy bag, contemplating the night ahead. She puts on her thermal leggings, down jacket and a hat, mindful of how cold she can get after a run, as warm muscles cool down and her body returns to its resting pace.

The breeze drops, the evening is calm and the sun sets while she sits against a rock brewing hot chocolate. As she gazes out west, the gloaming arrives, that short period of wonder when the light has not fully gone with the sun. The sky, a golden pink on the horizon, blends upwards into purples, blues and then to dark grey.

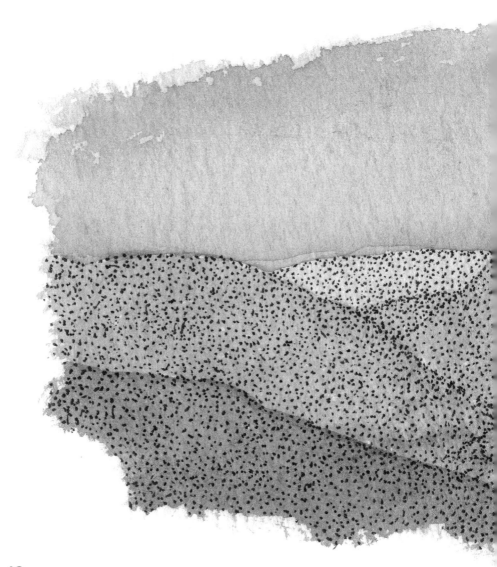

Sunset at Charnley Cairn

Suddenly she realises she is not alone. A man and dog are following the rough path from Esk Pike along the shallow ridge down towards Mosedale and Great Moss. She is slightly hidden from them by the rock she sits against, about twenty metres from the path.

If the dog has smelt her it ignores her, intent as it is on its own journey. In the half-light, the green of her bivvy bag blends in with the land; if the man notices her, he does not acknowledge her. Instinctively though, she winds down the dial on her stove, its blue flame extinguished as the gentle hiss of the releasing gas is stopped. The man strides out along the path. The dog runs slightly ahead, every now and then looking back to check the man is still following.

Holding her breath as they pass, she checks her fears. She'd had the conversation with a friend a few days before – of course it would be perfectly safe to sleep on the fell by herself, safer than walking down the street in broad daylight, where is the risk? She had felt angered by the conversation; not by her friend's concern, but in the way her freedom felt curtailed by the pressure not to put herself in such perceived danger.

The funny thing is that she doesn't feel in any kind of danger from these two. They are clearly following their own trod and, in the dim light of the gloaming, their presence feels almost spiritual. Together they make their way down the fell, moving into the darkness that's falling faster in the valley.

As their outlines fade she relights her stove, the hot chocolate soon bubbling and warm to drink. It is properly dark now; she is ready for sleep.

In the morning, after a breakfast of flapjack and coffee, she will pack up her kit and make her return journey to Eskdale, this time over the Scafells, Slight Side, following the Terrace Route back into the valley.

Before then she has a night of solitude and peace in this beloved place. How will she sleep? Probably fitfully, a combination of excitement, feeling a little cold, and an edge of nervousness she chastises herself for. No matter. Nights like these are so rare and special they are wasted in sleep. Snuggling down into her pit, she gazes up to the stars. There are always so many more in the mountains.

"Painting a landscape leads you to look so much.
When you return it feels like an old friend."

Upper Eskdale

Dawe

47

As Water Flows – Part 2

Geoff

Swinsty Gill and Lingcove Beck, no longer just names
but silver ribbons that rise beyond my map,
dancing steps among dry stone walls that
channel the valley through folds and gathering pens.
A baffling maze to all but a shepherd's eye,
before deep-lanes become ready guides
to the warmth of welcome at a hostel door.

And on I flow
as water flows,
drinking deeply.

Eskdale twists in cramped and airless folds,
dry-walled valley under low-browed trees.
To the cooler air of Slight Side's flanks
caught in deep shadows of boulder and crag.
A welcome breeze on a broad grass ridge
that beckons a runner to greater pace.
Too soon the cairn on Scafell's top.

And on I flow,
as water flows,
swift and smooth.

A compass line, an eastward choice,
the shadowed rocks of a summer beck
to the perfect jewel of Foxes Tarn.
Then spill into Mickledore's boulder blast
all shimmering airs and rising dust,
yet lark-voiced steps to Scafell Pike;
man-crafted island, anchored to the sky.

And on I flow,
as water flows,
echoes of the past.

Shin-scrape, pecking-step, boulder fields
Broad Crag, Ill Crag and then Great End
reluctant summits for a different day.
Back to the map at Esk Hause shelter
checking the height of a traverse line,
below Esk Pike on a careful bearing
to lay my hands on the Charnley Cairn.

And here I pause
to share his view.
Gratitude pools.

*View north from the
summit of Scafell*

8 Map Reading

Heather

It took many years for me to get to a place where I could read a map.

By this I don't mean being able to follow the lines of a path, trail or road to a

destination.

That's easy.

Years of failing,
   losing myself,
      going in the wrong direction,
         working out what the hell I had done
and subsequently finding myself.

Where I was on the hill.

Years of learning how to see, taking the time to understand.

Today, while I have more to learn, I understand better.

By 'read a map' I mean to be able to see
the shape of the mountains a map
depicts in three dimensions.

To interpret the swirls of its contours to the
extent that I can almost feel the mountains'
shape and demeanour.

Their impression in my head translates to
the world around me
(if I am not surrounded by mist).

I place myself and follow an imagined line on the ground to my
destination, all the time feeling for the behaviour of the land, making
sure the ways it rises and falls concurs with the map and so I always
know where I am.

In my mind's eye, when I read a map of mountains, they rise up from
the paper plane to form
                                    peaks,
                                        passes,
                                            valleys
 and other physical features.

Is it the same for others?
        I have asked and some do,
                                    some don't.
                                        It's a subjective thing,

My mathematical mind always wants to make patterns and shapes.
For contours to make sense to me I had to realise this and allow my
mind to wander in that kind of way.

Maps are one of the places where mathematics and art meet.

Cartography – the practice of making maps –
                                    is as much an art as it is a science.

            At least I think that's how it should be,

I think over the past century or so we've gone too far into the realms
of science and lost a few things along the way.

                        In painting maps I am definitely moving
                        into the artistic space of my mind.

        I would not recommend that anybody should try to
        navigate with a copy of one of my painted maps.

    Their accuracy is secondary to my paintbrush and mood.

        Painting a map of mountains I love leads me
            to value them even more.

Pinnacle Bield

Gerry Charnley Round, 2015, Late May Bank Holiday, Attempt 2

Geoff

I step out of the van into a car park already warm, despite the early hour. It's only three weeks since I was last here for our doomed, but eventful, GCR attempt and this feels like a very different day: summer's here and the Lake District is showing her best face. I'm on my own this time, after the kicking we took last time there seems precious little appetite across the team for another round. My running plans say that it needs to be today so I have decided that a solo, unsupported attempt is on the cards. It feels refreshingly uncomplicated. The last time gave me the information I needed about my fitness and attitude, so it's a 'turn up and run it' approach this time.

I check my time, touch the bridge wall at Elterwater and once more head off down that silent echoing lane. No mistake this time, right at the first junction and up the quarry ramps to the iron gate. My heart rate leaps as a figure jumps up from the stone shelter;

he's heavily wrapped in blankets and a cloud of dope fumes and almost sends me back to the van for a change of underwear. Either the adrenaline surge or the fumes give me a boost and I'm soon at Lingmoor summit. I note the time, then drop to the once-more perfect mirror of Blea Tarn. Blisco is still wet, but that's almost welcome as the heat is starting to build.

The same joyous dash down Eskdale, though a few less 'whoops' and no shared laughs. No time for tea at the hostel; I'm moving fast and I want to get as much in the bag before the heat of the day. A gentle and welcome breeze on Slight Side, so unlike the last time I was here. Scafell, then the welcome shade of Foxes Tarn gully. People already sunbathing on the shimmering cairn atop Scafell Pike.

The dry paths and boulders through to Great End throw up dust and heat. I'm conscious of drinking lots and I'm worried that I can't replenish water until the descent to Angle Tarn. I can feel my pace dropping.

I smile as I hit the traverse to the Charnley Cairn exactly, though I can't afford any self-congratulation having got myself in such a dehydrated state. A small stream before Angle Tarn allows me to relax a little as I fill both bottles; I don't want to risk taking water from the larger streams where I can see so many people. It's hot now, and the crowded path back up towards Sprinkling Tarn is hard on the feet and ears, but it's quieter as I turn for the steep pull onto Allen Crags. The stretch from the top of Allen Crags across to Borrowdale Valley is my least favourite part of this Round. It's broken ground and I find it hard to establish any rhythm in my running. There are three checkpoints along here so you have to keep map in hand and concentrate; I've got to resist the temptation to relax too soon, before I'm back down in the valley.

It's clear that I'm tiring in this heat and my pace has dropped even further. Through the late afternoon I run up the lane to Borrowdale Youth Hostel and I'm thinking I need to get a grip on this otherwise I'm not going to finish. The idea of an unsupported Round goes out of the window and I order assorted fizzy drinks and cakes, emergency treatment for dehydration and tiredness. Acknowledging the very real danger of not getting up again, I sit on a picnic bench under the trees and hoover up sugar and cold liquid – fast.

I have to confess that I'm sifting through the options, but the van is back in Elterwater and the easiest way to get there is to follow the route, at least as far as the Langdales, and by then it'll be just as easy to complete the route than take the steep drop into the valley. These are the mind games we play on long routes – tried and tested tactics to beat the negativity of a tired mind and reluctant legs. So it's off down Langstrath in golden evening light; no point in rushing as this is going to be slow and there will be enough light to run until late.

Langstrath is golden and gorgeous, warm and silent in the early evening, decent running even on tired legs. The sugar has kicked in and I'm now well hydrated so even the Stake Pass zigzags are not too unwelcome. I say hello to distinct and familiar trees and soon I'm at the tarn checkpoint, setting the compass for the bearing that will avoid the worst of the bogs on the climb to Thunacar Knott. It feels like a long climb and I stray off the bearing slightly, having to compensate as the top comes into sight. I know the Round is in the bag now, barring accidents, but I've still got one big decision to make.

Thorneythwaite Bridge

Descending Blea Rigg is some of the most runnable terrain in the Lake District: grassy, sheep-cropped turf that descends gently all the way. I can't fully relax though – I know there are two checkpoints to collect and a lot of confusing paths that aren't on the map, but this is easy going even at the end of a long day. As Silver Howe rises in front of me I have some decisions to make about the descent to High Close Youth Hostel, a wrong choice here could put me in head-high bracken. The maze negotiated, I'm safely on the road. I touch the gates of the hostel, then turn back the way I've come for the steep tarmac descent into Elterwater – it's a final insult to tired quads, but soon I'm among the stone cottages of the village.

I draw a few glances from the drinkers on the grass outside of the Britannia as I trot to the bridge and the finish of my day. The river looks too good to resist so it's through the gate, throw down my pack on the grassy bank, and lie down in the cold laughing water. I contemplate a beer, then reject that idea for the food that's waiting in the van. A slow walk to the car park and a satisfied smile, a lovely day out and a route to be enjoyed and respected.

As Water Flows – Part 3

Geoff

Skirting bogs and vaulting becks to
bright crowds and noise by Angle Tarn
into contrast silence on Allen Crags.
No chance of rhythm on broken ground
just a weary focus on step and line,
begrudging a nod to the course-setter's craft
checkpoints elusive as a runner tires.

And on I flow,
as water flows,
tired pools.

The anvil ring of the Borrowdale road
a last few steps to the hostel door.
Double drinks and a range of cakes
on a shaded bench under birdsong trees.
Study the map and schedule times,
elusive numbers for a tired mind.
Langstrath Valley welcomes weary legs.

And on I flow,
as water flows,
back to the hills.

Black Moss Pot and Tray Dub bridge
gentle running in the valley bed.
Familiar trees mark Stake Pass rising
unrelenting, steep, unwelcome,
to Thunacar Knott, then a choice to make.
The steep broken shoulder of Pavey Ark
or the grassy traverse under Sergeant Man?

And on I flow,
as water flows,
closing on the sea.

Hard-founded hills soften and shimmer
in the gold-wash close of a summer's day
only sheep break the silence of deserted fells.
A sun-tight skin and sweat turned to crystals
Blea Rigg turf under weary feet.
A last chance of water from a rock-pooled beck
then a maze of bracken to the High Close door.

And on I flow,
as water flows,
into the night.

A last hard road-mile, cruel on the legs,
to the same sleeping village where I awoke.
Happy drinkers in the Britannia garden
laughing as I lie down in the river bed,
a cold, quiet moment for thought and reflection.
A day spent alone, yet the company was good
map and compass, familiar fells, and Gerry's ghost.

And at the close,
one thing I know,
this day was mine.

*The shelter at
Esk Hause*

And what did he offer, the man who gave this gift?
Who strung these pearls on so fine a thread?
A seductive line through Lakeland's beauty
elusive yet precise, like him perhaps?
A twilight kingfisher half-seen through trees of time.
His open hand offers a lesson, simple yet priceless
"Learn to flow and these hills are yours."

And on he flows,
as water flows.
Eternal.

Why Traceless?

Heather

Traceless. These words mean leaving no physical trace, no sign that you have been somewhere. Almost as importantly these days for me it means leaving no data, no digital artefacts that show you have been somewhere. How far you have been, how fast you were going, where you were, who you were with. I prefer to keep my data private, just as I prefer to think for myself in the mountains, using a map and compass to guide my way, rather than the increasingly ubiquitous GPS.

Luddite? Maybe. I am also someone who innovates with data. I know what I can do with your data and I watch as humanity passes over its problem-solving abilities (the thing that underpins our abilities to learn and be creative) to machines and artificial intelligence, some of which I code. We are getting progressively stupider, a backwards evolution towards what at the very best leads to a more mundane life.

But fell running is anything but mundane. Gerry Charnley knew that.

For me, two of the core elements in fell running are its simplicity and honesty. Running over rough terrain in the mountains takes you to places that always challenge you physically and at times mentally while throwing such beauty at you that it's enough to blow your mind. Entirely absorbing, a world away from the ordinary. Simple in that it's putting one foot in front of the other as fast as you are capable of, or want to go. Honest because there are no hiding places.

In running with a map in your hand, navigating as you go, you have an all-encompassing experience. When the navigation is tricky I find complete physical and mental absorption with the problem in hand. Problem-solving with my own mind while coping with the physical challenges thrown at me by the mountainside – the climbs, descents, scree, bog, streams, boulders. All the while surrounded by beauty and sometimes I even get to run on a path. What is not to love?

While I never knew Gerry Charnley I am attracted to his Round, his history, and what I hope we could increasingly call his legacy because of the principles it espouses. Leave the GPS at home, don't use a tracking device. Just get out into the fells with your map and compass, enough kit to be safe and choose for yourself where you go. Think for yourself, visit some of the lesser-trod places. With the ability to take care of yourself in the hills comes the capacity to be creative and bold, to choose lines you would otherwise never have looked at.

Taking responsibility for your choices in the mountains, being self-sufficient, leaving no trace. The inspiration I take from Charnley's mindset and principles in the mountains tally with my own.

Tell them where you're going, but don't tell them where you've been.

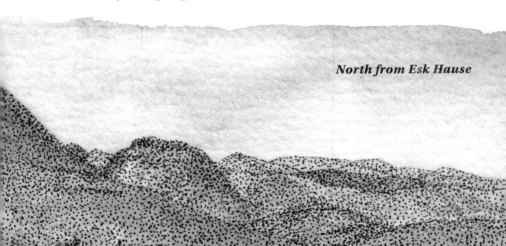

North from Esk Hause

Why Traceless?

Geoff

Here I must make a confession: moving through the hills in a way that might be considered 'traceless' has never come easy to me. It takes effort to leave behind the gear and devices that are offered up to the hollow promise of 'making mountain-going easier'. It is a temptation to instantly let people share my mountain journeys: there's an accidental, though lingering tendency to become part of conversations that stray towards 'crushing a climb, conquering a peak or smashing out a great route'.

But, like adventurers through the ages, I've more recently looked for a different kind of challenge, and this search has led me to some deep insights about the nature of challenge itself. By thinking about my relationship with upland areas I've begun to recognise a different way for me to be when I'm doing the things I love. I've moved from an adversarial position 'man against the mountain' to a 'low-impact, low-presence' position that captures what 'traceless' is all about.

I am not anymore a young man; I've had decades of exploring upland areas around the world, and, as I've tried to simplify my hill-going, I've begun to recognise that these 'new' experiences are not really new after all, they are the experiences that led me to venture into the hills in the first place. The days when gear was simple and the safety net was thin, when adventures were accessed by word of mouth and shared within close-knit communities of common interest.

For me this has been an interesting return, not least in remembering the things that I had forgotten.

The pride that I derive from spending self-sufficient hours and days moving quickly through remote territory, leaving no trace of my passage.

The satisfaction of accurately navigating my way through potentially dangerous terrain, with all of my senses attuned to the task, needing no recourse to the safety blanket that is the digital handrail of GPS.

The pleasure I take from a network of relationships with those who make their homes in remote places, wildlife and farm life, those who work here and those who maintain it for the pleasure of others.

The deep immersion in the slow change of nature, through the seasons, across the years, and in the accommodations that become necessary as I move into my later years.

All of these add up to a profoundly satisfying sense of being totally present every step of my journeys in the hills, part of an environment, rather than being possessed of the attitudes and equipment that cocoon me from the vagaries of the environment.

Ask people why, and how, they go to the hills, and a consistent response is that they go 'to get closer to something'. The 'something' varies widely, it may be nature, freedom, friends or 'my limits', yet none of these are brought any closer by adopting a high-tech/high-impact approach. Whether your desire is contained in an hour strolling along a lakeshore path, or expeditioning into remote ranges, you will inevitably be closer to the true essence of your experience without the insulation of 'stuff'. We desire the experiences that are intense and immediate, visceral and personal: simultaneously we distance ourselves from them by wrapping them in the unnecessary.

It takes a degree of confidence, and an appreciation of possible consequences, to go out into nature in a self-reliant way. Gerry Charnley understood this and demonstrated through his life and practice that to be safe one has to develop a particular set of skills. These are skills that many would see as archaic in these days of hand-held technology and naive belief that one can always rely on others to sort out the mess. Yet the acquisition of these skills can be a joy in itself – learning to map-read, understanding mountain conditions and weather, living comfortably off-grid, all offer wonderful opportunities to share and learn with others. Part of the legacy that Gerry left us is a system of access to these skills and experiences – the teachers and knowledge are out there for all.

12 Traceless Days

Geoff

I will give myself
to the grey mists and
they will deliver me
to the silent places,
where all my being is folded
into a lonely raven's croak.
My passing?
Only the sound of shoes on stone.

Long days alone,
and long days shared
with others.
Days when we have watched
the summer crowds
return to valley, car and pub,
yet we have stayed,
intent on further hills
now washed in golden
evening light
and the silence
of trails abandoned
to those who do not
plan their route
to close when the day
begins to fade.

For we are runners in
the wild places.
Our steps weave the seam
where fells meet sky.
Our senses tuned to
the outline of distant hills.
We weave a passage
through untracked hills.
We seek to leave no trace,
yet these journeys
mark us with
deep-etched memories
of friends and fellow travellers.
Rain, winters,
first light on dark hills,
the satisfaction of
a map close-followed
to open, lonely summits
or the secure folds
of tarn and valley.

We have learned the lessons
that these hills can teach
of humility, lasting pain,
loss and self-doubt.

We have gone beyond
the need to value our days
in terms of conquest.

For each of us
will remember our traceless days
with a deep and subtle pride.
Yet this pride is but a small thing,
when measured against
the freedom of the wild
and the company of hills.

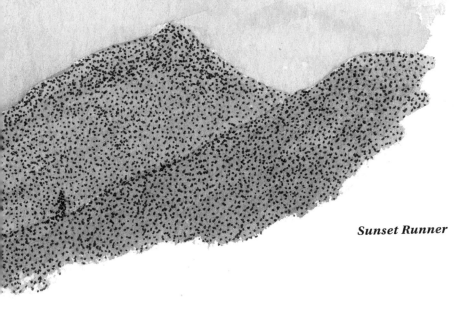

Sunset Runner

Acknowledgements

Geoff: It takes a certain boldness, even perversity, to undertake a heartfelt collaboration with someone who is almost a stranger. Jointly writing *Traceless* wasn't just about getting words and images to work together, it was about Heather and I ceasing to be strangers. We discovered that we are very different characters, but, like a human Venn diagram, there is common ground, a place of growing friendship, respect and interest.

That place is where this book was born.

Heather: Having a shared love of fell running was part of it. I think also that Geoff and I are both used to the, at times, perverse places that pushing yourself in the mountains can take you. I find problem-solving in the hills gives me a greater confidence for problem-solving and being creative in other parts of my life. While I can't say for sure, I think this may be true for Geoff too. Working with him made this project a joy. Our ideas bounced off each other and grew – we both think the result is better for it.

Geoff: Nobody anticipated Covid-19. Before lockdown we met once to talk about how to write together, then, like most people, we were forced online. What that means is that we are both incredibly grateful to our respective families who have offered nothing but support and tolerance through an extended creative process.

Deep thanks are due to Andy Jackson, friend, runner, and a photographer of great talent, for permission to use images from his Gerry Charnley Round.

Further thanks are due to Jo Allen of LastWord for editing our manuscript in a manner which was always sensitive, accurate and good-humoured.

That this book is so elegant is, to a very great extent, down to the vision and talents of Rhiannon Hughes of The Yorkshire Wordwright who is responsible for adding beauty, structure and form to our often vague ideas.

Heather: This is the fourth book I've made with Jo and Rhiannon. I have grown to love the making process with them, as a manuscript takes shape I become giddy with anticipation at what it will look like. Their enthusiasm and hard work is reflected in *Traceless*, and, as Geoff says, this is a far better book for Rhiannon's creative design and Jo's sensitive editing.

Thanks and acknowledgements also go to Harvey's Maps, who kindly gave us permission to reproduce parts of their Gerry Charnley Round map.